REBEL GIRLS CHAMPIONS

25 TALES OF UNSTOPPABLE ATHLETES

www.rebelgirls.com

Some of the artwork in this book has been previously published in the books Good Night Stories for Rebel Girls and Good Night Stories for Rebel Girls 2.

Created by Francesca Cavallo and Elena Favilli
Text by Abby Sher, Sarah Parvis, Sam Guss, Nana Brew-Hammond, Susanna Daniel, Jestine Ware, and Sonja Thomas
Art direction by Giulia Flamini
Cover illustrations by Annalisa Ventura
Graphic design by Annalisa Ventura and Kristen Brittain

Printed in Canada, August 2021
10 9 8 7 6 5 4 3 2 1
ISBN: 978-1-953424-08-2

CONTENTS

FOREWORD

Dear Rebels,

As a child, my parents were eager to find a sport for me to play—one with a modest uniform to accompany my hijab. That's how we found fencing. I loved everything about it, from the speed and strength to the carefully planned strategy of the sport. But sometimes, it was lonely. None of the other fencers looked like me. There were few other Black or brown athletes on the fencing team and definitely no other Muslim girls in hijab. But I didn't let that stop me.

What I loved most about fencing was the thrill of getting better. After I graduated from Duke University, I chased the dream of one day becoming the first woman of color to compete for the US National Team in sabre. I started from the bottom, with no experience on the senior level and certainly no experience on the World Cup circuit. I challenged myself to get better and to change the sport I loved. I went from being a young 20-something qualifying for my first US World Championship Team in Paris, France, to becoming one of the best fencers in the world.

As a five-time world medalist and world champion, the true peak of my career came in 2016, when I qualified for my first Olympic team. I had a unique opportunity to change the narrative about the Muslim community and challenge the way people viewed us. That summer at the Rio Olympic Games, I became the first woman in hijab to represent the United States and the first Muslim American woman to win an Olympic medal. I have proved the impossible is possible. Now I hope that young kids who look like me—kids with brown skin and who maybe wear hijab— know that there is space for them in any sport they love.

And that's why I love books like this—books that celebrate women in sports. *Rebel Girls Champions* showcases women from all over the world playing many different sports—and each story gives readers examples of focus, determination, and sportsmanship. Readers can enjoy stories about their favorite athletes, like Sky Brown, Chloe Kim, and Serena Williams. And they can meet new role models, like Ishita Malaviya, the first female surfer in India, and Lina and Sanna El Kott Helander, who are happiest when testing their endurance, running high up in the mountains. Readers can also revel in the stories of Hidilyn Diaz and Ariarne Titmus, just a couple of the women who made headlines during the Tokyo Olympics in 2021.

I know from experience the amount of hard work and commitment it takes to reach the top of your sport as an athlete. And I know what it's like to use your platform for good and to fight for social justice and other causes you believe in. Seeing athletes compete, break records, and achieve new heights is incredible. And seeing them take a stand—for their mental health and equal treatment—is even better. Simone Biles, Megan Rapinoe, Allyson Felix, and other athletes are paving the way for a new generation of young women. Athletes like the ones in this book inspire us—and teach us lessons for success in sports and in life.

Whether you play sports just for fun or you are training hard for a competition, know that you are always welcome in any sport you want to play. Know that, with practice, you will get better. You will get stronger. You will become faster. Know that your potential is limitless. Carry that knowledge with you on and off the field. It will change your life and help you as you serve others and speak up for the things you believe in.

Together, we can make the world a more inclusive and equitable place.

—Ibtihaj Muhammad

ALICE MILLIAT

ROWER

nce upon a time, women weren't allowed to compete in the Olympic Games. The president of the International Olympic Committee (IOC) declared that sports were too "violent" and inappropriate for ladies. *That's ridiculous,* thought Alice. She knew that women were strong and fast—and competitive too.

Born in France in 1884, Alice studied to become a teacher and translator. But what really made her feel alive was playing sports. Swimming, hockey, and rowing helped her body grow stronger and her mind grow sharper. And she knew she wasn't the only one. Sports were good for everybody!

In 1919, Alice asked the IOC to include women in the track and field program. They said no. So she started her own organization, the Fédération Sportive Féminine Internationale (FSFI). Three years later, they organized a big one-day sporting event just for women.

Around 20,000 fans came to watch 11 events in a stadium near Paris. Athletes from Czechoslovakia, France, Switzerland, the United Kingdom, and the United States ran, jumped, and threw shot puts and javelins. By the end of the day, 18 world records were broken! Four years later, Alice organized the games again, calling it the Women's World Games. They had a special opening ceremony with 3,000 carrier pigeons released into the sky! The IOC wanted Alice to stop the games immediately. This time, it was her turn to say no. She would not back down until women were allowed in the Olympics.

It took more than 70 years for Alice's dream to come true. By that time, Alice, the FSFI, and the Women's World Games were long gone. But today, every woman who steps into an Olympic arena has Alice to thank.

MAY 5, 1884–MAY 19, 1957

FRANCE

ILLUSTRATION BY
JULIETTE LÉVEILLÉ

"I CAME UP AGAINST A SOLID
WALL OF REFUSAL, WHICH LED
DIRECTLY TO THE CREATION OF
THE WOMEN'S OLYMPIC GAMES."
—ALICE MILLIAT

ALLYSON FELIX

SPRINTER

Once upon a time, there was a girl who ran so fast she could outrace the wind. Her name was Allyson.

She took up running in her freshman year of high school, where some teammates called her Chicken Legs. Her limbs may have been long and thin, but they sure were powerful!

Soon, she was sprinting all over the world! Between the Athens, Beijing, London, and Rio Olympic Games, she won nine medals.

In 2018, Allyson decided to become a mother. She was so excited. But about eight months into her pregnancy, she realized that something wasn't right. Allyson had to have emergency surgery to deliver her daughter early.

This surgery saved both of their lives.

Allyson couldn't do much while she recovered. She could barely walk for 30 minutes at a time. She started thinking a lot about Black mothers. They died in childbirth at a much higher rate than other women. Allyson decided to speak out. She told her story to members of the US Congress and asked them to act. Allyson knew that words and actions mattered. When a sponsor wanted to pay her less after she became a mom, she acted. She found a new sponsor. Then, she started her own sneaker company!

In 2021, Allyson went to Tokyo for her fifth Olympic Games. With her fierce determination and strong stride, she did it again! She won two more medals—in the 400 meter sprint and 400 meter relay.

It had been a challenging journey from pregnancy to the Olympic podium and from athletics to activism. Standing next to her teammates, draped in an American flag, Allyson said, "I'm absolutely where I'm supposed to be."

BORN NOVEMBER 18, 1985

UNITED STATES OF AMERICA

ILLUSTRATION BY
KIM HOLT

"I REALLY WANT
MY LEGACY TO BE
ONE OF SOMEONE
WHO FOUGHT FOR
WOMEN."
—ALLYSON FELIX

ARIARNE TITMUS

SWIMMER

Ariarne grew up surrounded by cool blue water. But when she was little, she preferred to play on land. On the Australian island of Tasmania, Ariarne—"Arnie" to family and friends—scampered around in the woods. Dressed up like a princess, she rode horses and built playhouses in the bush with her sister.

It was only when she turned seven that the water began to call her.

Arnie jumped right in, but she wasn't a very good swimmer at first. She spent countless hours in the pool. And by age 12, she was winning races.

When she got so good that no one in Tasmania could beat her, Arnie's parents had to make a tough decision. Should they stay on their island, where they had a beautiful home, great jobs, and kids happy at school? Or pack up and move to Queensland so Arnie could pursue her dream?

They chose Queensland, and a new adventure began. By 16, Arnie was Australia's reigning swim champion for girls under 18. Just two years later, she was ready for an even bigger pool—an Olympic-sized one.

In 2021, Arnie stood on a block at the end of a pool at the Tokyo Games. Next to her was Katie Ledecky, the world's fastest female swimmer. Arnie grasped the edge of the platform and focused. Her heart raced. A buzzer sounded, and she was off! For 3 minutes and 28 seconds, she trailed behind Katie. But in the last 28 seconds, Arnie shot ahead. She won the gold! Two days later, she won again, this time breaking an Olympic record.

Now when Arnie wants to dress up, she has something far better than princess gowns. She has two gold medals, a silver, and a bronze—bright, shiny reminders of her big dreams and hard work.

BORN SEPTEMBER 7, 2000

AUSTRALIA

ILLUSTRATION BY
SOL COTTI

"GOING INTO A RACE, WHAT I'VE
DONE IN TRAINING GIVES ME THE
CONFIDENCE THAT I CAN PERFORM."
—ARIARNE TITMUS

BRIGETTE LACQUETTE

ICE HOCKEY PLAYER

By the time Brigette was five years old, she was already on a mission. She wanted to join a hockey team. But that wasn't so easy for a little girl in the small First Nations community of Mallard, Manitoba. About four hours northwest of the city Winnipeg, Mallard had a firehouse, a water pump, and fewer than 120 people. What it didn't have was a hockey rink.

Lucky for Brigette, she had a family who saw the spark in her. They recognized her talent when she laced up her skates and chased her brothers across the ice. So her father flooded the backyard and built her a rink, right on the family lawn. And when she joined the closest team (it was still far away), her whole family pitched in to get her to practices and games.

As a child, Brigette developed eczema, an uncomfortable skin condition. When it flared up, she would itch like crazy! Some kids bullied her, making fun of her blotchy, irritated skin. But when Brigette suited up for hockey practice, her gear covered her like armor and protected her from the taunts of her classmates.

She shined on the ice! Even as a teenager, she made powerful shots and mapped out clever paths so she could zip past the opposing defense. But she wasn't always accepted. At 12 years old, playing in her first big tournament, she heard words that stung. *Go back to the reservation*, spat an opponent. Another called her a nasty name. Shocked and hurt, she looked to her father for advice. "Beat them on the ice," he said.

Brigette took her father's advice and didn't look back. She played in college and competed in the World Championships. And, in 2018, she was the first First Nations player on the Canadian women's Olympic hockey team.

BORN NOVEMBER 10, 1992

CANADA

"I FEEL LIKE I'VE OPENED A LOT OF DOORS, ESPECIALLY FOR THE LITTLE GIRLS WATCHING BACK HOME."
—BRIGETTE LACQUETTE

ILLUSTRATION BY MAYA MCKIBBIN

CHARLOTTE WORTHINGTON

BMX CYCLIST

Charlotte loved anything on wheels. Her first wheels were attached to a scooter. She scooted everywhere. Other kids made fun of her, calling her names like Scoots McGee. They just didn't get her.

At the skate park, Charlotte found other people who loved wheels as much as she did. She made new friends and discovered all sorts of new sports. But the sport that caught her eye was freestyle BMX. It was thrilling to watch! In BMX, cyclists ride around an obstacle course flipping off ramps and performing tricks. Their runs are scored on creativity, technique, height, and difficulty. Charlotte could do some tricks on her scooter, but BMX was on another level. *Maybe I need bigger wheels* . . . she thought.

After college, Charlotte worked as a cook in a Mexican restaurant and rode her bike in her off-hours. She got really good—really fast. A lot of the skills she'd been doing on her scooter also worked on a bike. But Charlotte was eager to land tricks that she'd never seen in competition before.

In 2021, BMX would be featured in the Olympics for the first time ever.

Charlotte trained for the Tokyo Games with one goal in mind: to pull off a 360 backflip and land herself on the Olympic podium. No woman had ever landed a 360 backflip in competition. Charlotte knew it was her ticket to a gold medal.

After flying high in the air on her first run, she crashed while landing and slid down the ramp on her side. But on her second run, she launched herself skyward, flipping and rotating in a perfect 360 backflip. She landed smoothly, making BMX history! Charlotte was the first Olympic gold medalist in women's freestyle BMX. She always knew she'd get further on wheels.

BORN JUNE 26, 1996

UNITED KINGDOM

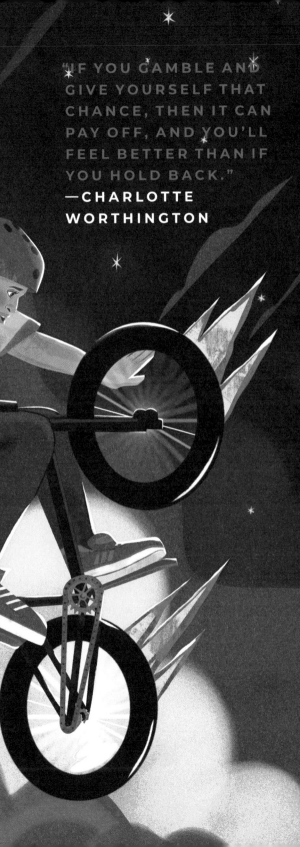

"IF YOU GAMBLE AND GIVE YOURSELF THAT CHANCE, THEN IT CAN PAY OFF, AND YOU'LL FEEL BETTER THAN IF YOU HOLD BACK."
—CHARLOTTE WORTHINGTON

ILLUSTRATION BY LYDIA MBA

CHLOE KIM

SNOWBOARDER

Once there was a girl named Kim Seon, but people called her Chloe. She loved hiking, spicy foods, and going on adventures with her family. One time, when Chloe was little, her dad drove through the night so they could go snowboarding just as dawn rose between the mountain peaks. He thought it would be a fun day trip. He had no idea that Chloe would one day become a legend on the slopes.

When she was just four years old, Chloe fell in love with snowboarding. Later, her parents sent her to live with an aunt in Geneva, Switzerland. There, she trained on the majestic mountains of the Alps.

"I literally set a goal for myself when I was 10," Chloe said. She vowed to compete in the X Games, a huge international extreme-sports competition. And she wanted to be the first girl to do back-to-back 1080s—that's six full rotations in the air! She set an impressive goal—and crushed it!

First, she became the youngest athlete ever to win a medal at the X Games. Next up were the Olympics in 2014, but the rules said she wasn't old enough to compete! The 2018 Olympics were extra special to Chloe. They were held in Pyeongchang, South Korea. Chloe's parents were born in Korea, so she felt like she had a chance to represent the United States *and* her Korean heritage.

Chloe had three runs to hit her best score. The first went smoothly. On the second, she fell. Then, as she sped down the mountain for the third time, she felt the energy of the crowd lifting her up. And she became the first woman to land two consecutive 1080s! With the wind in her hair and her smile sparkling against the snowy landscape, Chloe became an Olympic champion. She set her sights high and leaped to meet them.

BORN APRIL 23, 2000

UNITED STATES OF AMERICA

ILLUSTRATION BY
SALINI PERERA

"IT'S LIKE A NEW
ADVENTURE EVERY TIME
YOU DROP INTO THE PIPE."
—CHLOE KIM

FLEUR JONG

PARALYMPIC LONG JUMPER AND SPRINTER

Once upon a time, there was a girl named Fleur who dreamed of flying. Not with wings—with blades.

Her quest to soar began just a few days before her 17th birthday. Fleur went home sick from school, thinking she had the flu. But it ended up being an infection so serious that her doctors had to amputate. She lost her right foot, part of her left foot, and eight of her fingertips. Later, she had surgeries to remove her legs below her knees. She was devastated.

Fleur missed her old body and life so much. But her friends and coaches convinced her she could have an incredible new life through sports. They were right. She began an adventure of discovery, learning how to walk, run, and race with her new body.

She hit the track with special blades attached to her legs. Within five years, she was sprinting past her competitors. And, in 2019, Fleur broke a world record in the 100 meter dash, racing to first place in just over 13 seconds. "Sprinting makes me feel like I can fly," said Fleur. "And if you can fly, you can go anywhere you like."

While Fleur was perfecting her sprinting skills, her coach and her teammates thought of a way for her to fly even farther: the long jump. Fleur considered it. Could she coordinate every muscle she had to jet her body into the air? Could she land safely on her blades?

She was terrified. But Fleur had soared past fear before.

A month later, she stood at the World Para Athletics Championships in Poland. Balanced on her blades, she began to run. At the jump line, she sprang off the ground and sailed into history. Fleur broke the long jump world record!

BORN DECEMBER 17, 1995

THE NETHERLANDS

"AN IMPAIRMENT DOES NOT HAVE TO BE A LIMITATION. YOU CAN DO SO MUCH MORE THAN YOU THINK."
—FLEUR JONG

ILLUSTRATION BY
MIA SAINE

HIDILYN DIAZ

WEIGHTLIFTER

Once upon a time, there was a tiny girl in Zamboanga, Philippines, who was as strong as a giant.

Hidilyn began weightlifting as a child. Whenever she found a piece of wood, she'd hoist it into the air. She carried gallons of water great distances from the well to her house. She may have been small, but metal hubcaps were no problem for Hidilyn! Even hefty cement blocks barely slowed her down. She could lift anything! When someone gave her a barbell to practice with, she trained with it until it fell to pieces.

Hidilyn joined the national weightlifting team when she was 17. She competed in two Olympic Games without winning any medals. At her third, she brought home silver. But Hidilyn was hungry for gold!

She was at an event in Malaysia when COVID-19 lockdowns began. *Oh no!* thought Hidalyn. *I'm stuck!* She couldn't go outside, see her family, or practice with her coaches at the gym. She trained indoors for two years, using weights made of water jugs tied to bamboo poles. Sometimes her homemade weights slipped out of her hands. They would land with a heavy thud. She worried she'd break the floor!

Hidilyn kept training. She wanted to win the gold at the 2021 Tokyo Olympics. But she was a little nervous. Could she do it?

She could—and she did. And she beat an Olympic record! The little girl who loved to lift won the Philippines its very first gold medal.

Hidilyn climbed onto the winner's podium with happy tears streaming down her face. She belted out her country's national anthem with pride.

BORN FEBRUARY 20, 1991

PHILIPPINES

ILLUSTRATION BY
DEANDRA HODGE

"I CANNOT QUIT
AFTER WINNING."
—HIDILYN DIAZ

ISHITA MALAVIYA

SURFER

When Ishita looked out at the ocean, she saw freedom and fun. But many people around her saw the ocean as something scary. In the busy coastal city of Mumbai, India, countless fishermen worked on the water. But many didn't know how to swim. To them, crashing waves were dangerous! But Ishita wasn't afraid. She daydreamed of one day traveling to California, where surfers rode the crests and curls of giant waves.

She got her chance much closer to home. While studying journalism in college, some friends put her on her first surfboard. It was like a brilliant sunset breaking through the clouds. "I remember smiling on my first wave all the way to shore and all the way back home from the beach," she said.

Hooked on the sensation of gliding above the waves, Ishita went to her computer and looked up "surfing in India." There were no results! At the time, there were only 13 pro surfers in the whole country of more than one billion people! And they were all men.

Ishita and her boyfriend saved every dime possible until they could buy a used surfboard. And once they had it, they had to take turns in the water. In the beginning, Ishita was battered by the waves, but she paddled out again and again, getting stronger with every day at the beach.

She and her boyfriend moved to a small seaside town and opened up a surf club. They earned money from tourists so they could offer free classes to the kids in the village. Rather than fearing the great open waters, the community could learn to swim and play right by their homes. Together with Ishita—the first female surfer in India—they could become guardians of the environmental wonders right outside their door.

BORN JANUARY 6, 1989

INDIA

"WHEN I AM ON MY LONGBOARD, I JUST FEEL LIKE I AM DANCING ON THE WATER."
—ISHITA MALAVIYA

ILLUSTRATION BY
ANDRESSA MEISSNER

KATE AND HELEN RICHARDSON-WALSH

FIELD HOCKEY PLAYERS

As a young girl, Kate was painfully shy. When Helen was young, she felt like she didn't fit in anywhere. Both girls grew up in the United Kingdom, and both started playing field hockey as kids. Neither of them knew that they'd one day stand on an Olympic podium, holding hands and making history together.

As a kid, Kate swore she'd never play hockey. But she changed her tune once she picked up a stick. Running down the field and defending her goal thrilled her. Hockey was always part of Helen's childhood. With her three older brothers, she practiced dribbles, pushes, and scoops. Other kids teased her for always playing with the boys, but for her, "nothing else mattered" when she was on the hockey field.

Kate and Helen were both picked to represent Great Britain at the Olympic Games in 2000. The team didn't bring home any medals that year, but for Kate and Helen, something else wonderful happened. They realized that they had a lot more in common than just a love of hockey.

A few years later, Kate and Helen started dating. And in 2013, they got married, surrounded by family, friends, and cupcakes.

After their wedding, Kate and Helen were more determined than ever to get back to the Olympics. It wasn't going to be easy. Kate was recovering from a broken jaw, and Helen had to have multiple surgeries on her back. But together, they pushed through. And in 2016, when their team scored the winning goal at the Olympics in Rio de Janeiro, Kate and Helen became the first same-sex married couple to win an Olympic gold as teammates.

KATE, BORN MAY 9, 1980 ◆ HELEN, BORN SEPTEMBER 23, 1981

UNITED KINGDOM

"MY HOPE FOR HOCKEY AND SPORT IS FOR WOMEN AND GIRLS TO BE SEEN AS EQUAL TO MEN, TO BE VALUED AND RESPECTED IN THE SAME WAY."
—HELEN RICHARDSON-WALSH

ILLUSTRATION BY
MONICA MIKAI

KATERINA STEFANIDI

POLE-VAULTER

Once there was a girl named Katerina whose parents wanted her to run fast and jump high, like they did when they were younger. Katerina didn't love running or jumping. She was pretty good at both and at gymnastics too. But one challenge at a time just wasn't that exciting for her.

One day, when Katerina was 10, she was watching the Olympics on TV. An athlete did something she'd never seen before. Carrying a long flexible pole, he sprinted toward a high bar. Just before he reached the bar, he planted the pole in the ground and catapulted himself into the air! When he flew high enough, he twisted over the bar and fell backward onto a soft mat. Katerina thought, *Now that's a sport that has it all—running, jumping, and twisting and tumbling like a gymnast. That would never get boring!*

Katerina gave pole-vaulting a try. And within a few years, she won the World Youth Championships!

As a teen, she trained with a coach who pressured her to lose weight. She developed an eating disorder and even gave up pole-vaulting for a while. But then, Katerina decided to make the sport fun for herself again. She found a new coach, and her joy returned. Katerina moved to the United States for college, where she became part of a tight-knit team. She got even stronger and healthier and went on to win gold at the 2016 Olympics.

Katerina found love in pole-vaulting—and with another pole-vaulter! She married a fellow athlete and made him her coach. Whenever Katerina doubts herself, he reminds her how talented she is. He's always by her side cheering her on as she runs, plants her pole, and launches herself into the air. "It's the closest one can come to flying by using their own powers," she says.

BORN FEBRUARY 4, 1990

GREECE

ILLUSTRATION BY
MONICA MIKAI

"YOU LEARN SO MUCH MORE
FROM YOUR BAD DAYS."
—KATERINA STEFANIDI

KIT DESLAURIERS

SKI MOUNTAINEER

Once there was a girl named Kit who was on top of the world—literally. She stood at the summit of Mount Everest, about to ski down the tallest peak on Earth. With ice all around her, she felt a bright heat wash over her. It was a mixture of excitement and determination—along with a healthy dose of fear. She'd been working toward this moment her whole life.

As a child, Kit was always into playing sports and seeking adventure. She was a runner, cyclist, rock climber, and skier. She was also fascinated by the different landscapes and species on Earth. *How*, she wondered, *did humans fit in?* When she was 10 years old, she heard that the Arctic National Wildlife Refuge in Alaska was being threatened because companies wanted to drill there for fossil fuels. She wanted to protect the land from drilling. *But how?*

After studying environmental political science in college, Kit joined a ski patrol, saving people from avalanches, rushing rivers, and steep cliffs. She also trained to be a competitive skier. In 2004 and 2005, Kit was named the world champion of freeskiing, which combines skiing with acrobatics!

Still, she had bigger plans. She wanted to be the first person to climb up and ski down all Seven Summits, which are the highest mountains on each continent. She'd tackled the first six and had one to go. That's how she wound up atop Mount Everest, gazing at that icy drop in awe. And she did it!

Even after she skied down, Kit knew she wasn't done exploring.

"Some people think it's all about adrenaline," she said. "But it's not." For Kit, it's about connecting to and honoring the raw beauty of the wilderness. Today, she leads expeditions into the Arctic National Wildlife Refuge to help measure the impact of climate change and protect the vast, untamed lands.

BORN NOVEMBER 23, 1969

UNITED STATES OF AMERICA

ILLUSTRATION BY
XUAN LOC XUAN

"I LEARNED EARLY ON
THAT WHEN I DON'T
HAVE MY SKIS, IT
JUST FEELS LIKE
SOMETHING'S MISSING."
—KIT DESLAURIERS

LINA AND SANNA EL KOTT HELANDER

SKYRUNNERS

Once upon a time, there were twin sisters named Lina and Sanna. They grew up in Åre, Sweden, surrounded by the towering Scandinavian Mountains. Lina and Sanna's outdoor adventures were legendary, filled with hiking, running, skiing, and cycling. They planted vegetables and picked berries, chased their dogs, and painted landscapes. They loved nature—especially the open sky.

One day, some of their friends invited them to go on a new adventure where they'd race up a huge mountain. Lina and Sanna paused. They knew it would be a big challenge. But of course they said yes!

At the starting line, they squeezed into a narrow trail crowded with runners. *Gross!* Lina thought as her face got way too close to a few people's armpits. But then they shot forward! As they ran higher, the pack thinned out, and Lina and Sanna felt like they were floating. The endless blue skies and the sparkling lake below inspired them to run even faster. They leaped past the finish line, flushed with excitement and hooked on this new sport: skyrunning.

Since 2016, Lina and Sanna have been bounding up mountains and winning medals at Skyrunner World Series races around the globe. They've also learned that this kind of racing can be very hard on their bodies. Sanna once fell into a freezing river during a race, and Lina has had two knee surgeries.

To take care of themselves and the animal population, they eat only plant-based foods and fuel themselves with vegetables, nuts, berries, and beans. Their motto is *Eat green, run mean*—which is exactly what they do!

BORN FEBRUARY 28, 1994

SWEDEN

30

"THIS IS WHAT I'M GOOD AT!
I FEEL LIKE A MOUNTAIN GOAT!"
—LINA EL KOTT HELANDER

ILLUSTRATION BY
JENNIFER BERGLUND

LISA LESLIE

BASKETBALL PLAYER

Once there was a left-handed girl named Lisa who was taller than her second-grade teacher. Kids called her names, but her mother encouraged her to be proud of her height.

Everyone asked Lisa if she played basketball. She hated that question. But she wanted to fit in, so she decided to try it out. Soon she learned to dribble and shoot right-handed like everyone else. Lisa kept training and became so good that more than 100 colleges reached out to her—before she even started high school!

The key to becoming a champion, she said, was setting goals. She wrote down her objectives and pinned them all over the house.

After thriving on the college courts, Lisa set her sights on the Olympics. Sadly, opportunities for women were limited. Men could play in the National Basketball Association (NBA). But there wasn't a US women's league yet. So Lisa played in Italy before earning her spot on the US Olympic team. In 1996, she won a gold medal at her first Olympic Games!

That same year, the NBA created a women's league, the WNBA, and Lisa joined the Los Angeles Sparks in 1997. Five years later, in front of cheering fans, Lisa caught a long pass and charged toward the basket. The announcer cried, "What is she going to do?" Just then, she made history as the first woman at a WNBA game to slam-dunk!

She won three Most Valuable Player awards and three more Olympic gold medals. Then, after 12 seasons, Lisa retired from basketball and set some new goals. A natural leader on and off the court, she completed her business degree and returned to the Sparks as an owner.

BORN JULY 7, 1972
UNITED STATES OF AMERICA

"I WANT TO PROVE
ONCE AGAIN, TO
EVERY LITTLE GIRL
OR BOY THAT HAS
GOALS AND WORKS
HARD, THAT THEY
CAN DO AND
ACHIEVE ANYTHING.
ABSOLUTELY
ANYTHING."
—LISA LESLIE

ILLUSTRATION BY
KIM HOLT

MARTA VIEIRA DA SILVA

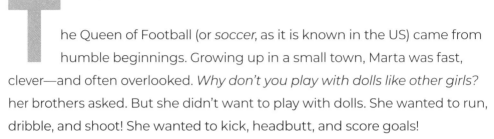

SOCCER PLAYER

The Queen of Football (or *soccer*, as it is known in the US) came from humble beginnings. Growing up in a small town, Marta was fast, clever—and often overlooked. *Why don't you play with dolls like other girls?* her brothers asked. But she didn't want to play with dolls. She wanted to run, dribble, and shoot! She wanted to kick, headbutt, and score goals!

When she didn't have a soccer ball, she used what she could find: old deflated balls or crumpled-up rags, paper, and plastic bags. Hunger, lack of running shoes, and grumpy older brothers did *not* slow Marta down.

At 14 years old, she embarked on a legendary journey. First stop: Rio de Janeiro. It took her three days on a bus to get there. And the huge bustling city was so different from her tiny rural town, she might as well have flown to Mars!

Marta laced up her sneakers and tried out for a professional soccer team. The coaches and the other players didn't know who she was. But after that day, they'd never forget. With laser focus and swift feet, she danced the ball past her opponents and slammed it into the goal again and again.

She got the job.

Later, she took her talents to Sweden and the United States, and of course, back home to Brazil. Playing in five World Cups, she scored more goals than any other player. She was even named Player of the Year six times!

Marta has scored more international goals than any other Brazilian player, male or female. But the Queen of Football knows her influence is more important than the goals she scores. It is in her message to girls everywhere: "Believe in yourself and trust yourself."

BORN FEBRUARY 19, 1986

BRAZIL

ILLUSTRATION BY
ANNALISA VENTURA

"I NEED TO BE ALL-IN.
EVERYTHING I DO,
IT'S 100 PERCENT."
—MARTA VIEIRA DA SILVA

MEGAN RAPINOE

SOCCER PLAYER

Once there was a girl named Megan who loved soccer, fashion, and family.

Megan grew up with lots of siblings in Redding, California. She started playing soccer when she was just four years old and soon proved to be very talented.

She was always looking out for her teammates and had amazing power in her passes. Sometimes, after blasting a ball into the goal, she would sing out to the crowd or raise up her arms, as if she were giving everyone watching a big hug. Megan's family loved celebrating her victories, but her mom reminded her that winning wasn't everything.

One of Megan's biggest triumphs on the field was in the 2011 World Cup. She kicked the ball 50 yards to Abby Wambach in overtime. Abby headed the ball into the net. The fans—and the team—went wild!

After that, Megan was a star player in the 2012 Olympics, the 2015 World Cup, the 2016 Olympics, and the 2019 World Cup.

Still, she kept thinking about what her mom told her and how she could use her skills and fame to help others. In 2012, Megan announced publicly that she was gay and that she believed everyone should have the right to get married. Four years later, she took a knee during the national anthem to protest racial injustice. She also spoke out for gender equality, leading the US Women's National Team to sue the US Soccer Federation for paying them less than male soccer players. When she scored the winning goal in the World Cup in 2019, the crowd chanted, "Equal pay! Equal pay!"

"Putting yourself out there is hard, but it's so worth it," she says.

BORN JULY 5, 1985

UNITED STATES OF AMERICA

"LIFT OTHER PEOPLE UP.
SHARE YOUR SUCCESS."
—MEGAN RAPINOE

ILLUSTRATION BY
KIM HOLT

MICHELLE KWAN

FIGURE SKATER

Once there was a girl who floated through fields of gold. Her name was Michelle. From the time she was five years old, she knew she wanted to be an ice skater. Sometimes she went to sleep in her skates so she could get on the ice before dawn. Every day, she practiced her leaps and lutzes, spins and stretches, trying out new moves. And at age six, she won her first competition.

Michelle's parents were thrilled but also concerned. They were both juggling multiple jobs while running a family restaurant. There was no money for sparkly costumes or brand-new skates. Michelle told them none of that mattered. Who needs fancy skates and sequins to land a double axel?

In 1991, when Nagano, Japan, was chosen to host the 1998 Olympics, Michelle got a sticker and put it over her bed. Every day for seven years, she looked at it before she closed her eyes at night and again first thing in the morning, visualizing herself there. Michelle not only got to the Olympics, but she also won a silver medal! Four years later, she went to the Olympics again. Her graceful performance mesmerized the audience. Even after she fell during one of her routines, she picked herself up and skated on, earning a bronze medal.

Michelle won more than 40 championships, including five world titles. But Michelle thought, *Medals don't really mean that much. It's the experience, the story of the skating, the love.*

As she sailed across the ice for her last Olympic program, set to the song "Fields of Gold," everyone could feel the love in every move she made.

BORN JULY 7, 1980
UNITED STATES OF AMERICA

"I DIDN'T LOSE
THE GOLD. I WON
THE SILVER."
—MICHELLE KWAN

ILLUSTRATION BY
LILY KIM QIAN

MIHO NONAKA

Miho's dad loved to climb mountains. And there are a lot of mountains in Japan, where Miho and her sisters grew up. Miho's dad decided to take the kids to train with him at the gym. Miho watched as her older sister clambered up the wall. Even though Miho had never climbed before, she had a new goal. She wanted to be a better climber than her sister!

With enough training, she knew she could do it.

Miho threw herself into her new sport. She dangled by her fingertips to strengthen her grip and spent hours stretching to further her reach. She discovered a type of climbing called bouldering. In bouldering, climbers don't use any ropes. They scramble up giant rocks—or indoor climbing walls designed to look like giant rocks—using nothing but their strength and their wits. Bouldering is all about strategy.

As Miho mastered her sport, she came up with a new goal: to be the best boulderer in the world.

In 2018, Miho won the overall bouldering title at the Climbing World Cup. Soon she set her sights even higher. In 2021, the Olympics would include sport climbing for the very first time. And Japan was hosting the games. This was Miho's chance to show off her skills!

But just before the Olympics, she hurt herself. When she arrived in Tokyo, her wrist and her knee were in intense pain. Even with her injuries, her strength and speed earned her a silver medal. She was proud to stand on the Olympic podium with the silver medal around her neck. But Miho is competitive by nature. Next time, she will go for gold.

BORN MAY 21, 1997

JAPAN

ILLUSTRATION BY
SALINI PERERA

"MY GOAL IS TO BECOME THE
WORLD'S GREATEST CLIMBER."
—MIHO NONAKA

SARAH FULLER

SOCCER PLAYER AND FOOTBALL PLAYER

Once there was a soccer star named Sarah who laced up her cleats and played like a girl. She could kick the ball 60 yards even when she was in high school! She was strong and smart and always cheered on her teammates. As a captain and goalie, she loved motivating her team.

Sarah dove for the ball, slid for saves, and earned a soccer scholarship to Vanderbilt University, where she planned to study medicine and get out on the field as much as possible. But just before she started school, she broke her foot and had to sit on the bench. Then she hurt her back . . . and later developed a stress fracture.

Her injuries were getting in the way of her plans! Even though she was angry and frustrated, Sarah realized something: when you play with a team, it isn't about you alone. So she refocused her energy on getting healthy and supporting her team. Her dream was to go to the Southeastern Conference tournament. In her senior year, she did just that—and her team won!

Soon after, Sarah got a call that changed her life. One of her coaches was on the line. He asked whether she wanted to be a kicker for Vanderbilt's football team. *Yes, of course!* she replied without hesitation.

As she stepped up to the ball, Sarah became the first woman ever to play in the Power Five, the highest level of college football. Two weeks after that, she ran to the ball and gave it a ferocious kick. When the ball sailed through the uprights, she became the first woman to score in a Power Five football game!

When reporters asked her about her success, Sarah said maybe it was because of her lucky socks. More likely, it was because of her awesome skills, her dedication, and her helmet that read "Play Like a Girl."

BORN JUNE 20, 1999
UNITED STATES OF AMERICA

ILLUSTRATION BY
CARMEN CASADO

"WE NEED TO BE
SUPPORTING ONE
ANOTHER. WE NEED
TO BE LIFTING
EACH OTHER UP.
THAT'S WHAT
A TEAM'S ABOUT."
—SARAH FULLER

SERENA WILLIAMS

TENNIS PLAYER

Once there was a girl named Serena who loved dressing up in tutus and speaking her mind. She was the youngest of five sisters who all shared a single bedroom in Compton, California. When she was three, her dad opened up a whole new world for her and her sister Venus. He taught them to play tennis.

He also asked some local kids to come by the public courts and boo at the girls while they practiced. That way, they'd learn how to focus and believe in themselves. It was the most important lesson of Serena's life.

The sisters were both very talented athletes who worked hard on their quick reflexes and mighty swings. Serena started playing tennis professionally when she was just 14 years old. Soon she was collecting titles and trophies all over the world. Sometimes she played doubles with Venus, and sometimes the sisters were paired off against each other in a match. No matter what, they always cheered each other on.

Serena has spent more than 300 weeks as the top-ranked woman in the world. She has also won the most Grand Slam singles titles of the modern era. And she is a powerhouse off the court too.

That lesson her dad taught her about believing in herself continues to guide her as she speaks out for human rights. She demands that all athletes are treated equally regardless of gender or skin color. She also created the Serena Williams Foundation to build schools in Jamaica and Africa.

As for those tutus she loves, her fashion line has clothes for all body types. Serena and her daughter, Olympia, can often be seen in matching frills, showing off their style and practicing their serves.

BORN SEPTEMBER 26, 1981
UNITED STATES OF AMERICA

"I'VE GROWN MOST NOT FROM VICTORIES BUT SETBACKS."
—SERENA WILLIAMS

ILLUSTRATION BY CAMILLA RU

SIMONE BILES

GYMNAST

Simone was a bubbly girl who loved shopping, pasta, and doing roundoffs, back handsprings, and double layouts. Her grandparents adopted her when she was very young. At six years old, she visited a gymnastics center on a daycare field trip. Standing on the sidelines, she started imitating what she saw. The coach sent home a letter saying Simone should start training with them.

Soon, her life revolved around the mats, vault, balance beam, and uneven bars. As she trained, she discovered she had a rare gift. She could always tell where she was in the air, even as she flipped and rotated.

By the time she was 14, Simone had won her first national competition. Two years later, she was the first Black girl to win gold in the all-around at the World Championships! In her bedazzled hot pink leotard, she lit up the entire arena with her breathtaking moves.

By the end of 2020, Simone had earned five Olympic medals and 25 world championship medals—many of them gold! If she put all her medals around her neck at once, she'd fall down! And she's always coming up with new ways to flip and soar. She even has four moves named after her!

At the Tokyo Olympics, something unexpected happened. She lost herself in the air. That could be dangerous for a gymnast like Simone. She decided she needed to take time to care for herself physically and mentally. She withdrew from most of her events and cheered for her teammates instead. When she returned for the final balance beam event, she won the bronze!

Because of her strength, skills, and sportsmanship, Simone is known as the "GOAT," or greatest of all time.

BORN MARCH 14, 1997

UNITED STATES OF AMERICA

ILLUSTRATION BY
ELINE VAN DAM

"ME BEING HAPPY OUTSIDE
THE GYM IS JUST AS IMPORTANT
AS ME BEING HAPPY AND DOING
WELL IN THE GYM."
—SIMONE BILES

SKY BROWN

SKATEBOARDER

When Sky was a baby, she liked to push her dad's skateboard around the house. It didn't take her long to discover that it was more fun to climb up on the board and whoosh across the floor.

She spent hours zooming around on the skate ramp her dad built in the backyard. Worried, her parents looked on. She was so small. They didn't want her to get hurt! Sky's dad even refused to teach her tricks. So when she got a bit older, she taught herself! She watched videos online and studied other skaters. They were all much bigger than she was, but she figured out how to make the moves work for her. She also noticed that most of the skaters were men. In fact, there weren't any other girls her age at the skate park at all. But Sky knew she could change that.

At 10 years old, she became the youngest professional female skateboarder in history. At 11, she competed in her first X Games. At this extreme-sports competition, fans watched and hoped to see something wild and new.

During her run at the X Games, Sky skated up and down the sides of the course, gaining speed and power. When she was ready, she threw back her right arm. With her left, she reached down to grab her board. She popped into the air and spun around 540 degrees. The crowd was amazed. Sky was the first girl to ever land a frontside 540 in a competition!

Two years later, Sky was the youngest athlete to represent Great Britain at the Summer Olympics. Landing a trick called a kickflip indy took her three tries. But she did it. Holding her bronze medal, Sky grinned. "It's like a dream," she said. Girls around the world had seen her land that trick. And maybe some of them were already outside, teaching themselves to skate like Sky.

BORN JULY 7, 2008
JAPAN AND UNITED KINGDOM

ILLUSTRATION BY
KATE PRIOR

SKATER

"IT DOESN'T MATTER
HOW OLD OR YOUNG
YOU ARE. YOU CAN
DO ANYTHING."
—SKY BROWN

SUNI LEE

When Suni was little, she loved to watch videos of girls doing gymnastics routines. She marveled at how they twirled and spun, stretched and posed, and flew through the air—like they had magic inside them. Suni believed the magic was inside her too.

Her father agreed, so he began to help her. He spotted her when she did backflips and jumped on the bed. He even built her a balance beam in the backyard.

But there were other kids in Suni's house. Suni took up so much space doing her routines that her mother finally declared that enough was enough. She enrolled Suni in gymnastics classes when she was six years old.

Suni grew up to be just like those girls in the videos she used to watch. She sailed over uneven bars, circling and swinging, balancing and turning, and landing with such grace that it all seemed easy. But the truth was, Suni's uneven bar routine was the most difficult in the world!

When Suni went to Tokyo in 2021, she became the first-ever Hmong American athlete to compete in the Olympics. The Hmong are an ethnic group from Asia. Suni's parents are Hmong refugees from Laos, and her family lives in Saint Paul, Minnesota. Their community is very important to them. Hundreds of Hmong friends and family gathered to watch Suni compete. They held their breath as she performed tricky moves and yelled with joy as her scores came in. She was the first Asian American gymnast to win a gold medal in the all-around event.

"This is my family's medal, my medal, my coach's medal," Suni said when she won.

BORN MARCH 9, 2003

UNITED STATES

"DO NOTHING MORE
AND NOTHING LESS . . .
MY NORMAL IS GOOD
ENOUGH."
—SUNI LEE

TEGAN VINCENT-COOKE

Once upon a time, there was a girl named Tegan who just wanted to fit in and do what everyone else her age could do. Tegan has quadriplegic cerebral palsy, which means her body gets stiff as a tree. It can be hard for her to move her arms and legs, and her muscles often spasm.

When Tegan was five years old, her parents took her to a horse-riding school near their home in Bristol, England. It was specially equipped for people with disabilities. "I loved it because I was with other people who didn't really fit in," said Tegan.

She felt free when she was riding—her muscles relaxed and stretched out. It was as if her body became one with the horse's as they moved together, played games, and bonded. What started as a hobby soon became so much more. After watching riders compete in the Paralympics, Tegan made an exciting decision: one day, she was going to compete too!

The sport she chose was dressage, which Tegan calls "ballet on a horse." Dressage is all about the relationship and training between a horse and a rider. Tegan gives her horse a series of calm but firm commands, and the horse responds. She and her horse have to trust each other and complete movements together so they flow like a smooth, choreographed dance.

When Tegan is not practicing with a horse, she makes fun videos explaining what it's like to live with cerebral palsy. As a public speaker, she inspires people to really look at and appreciate one another.

She's won many titles already, but she is determined to be the first Black woman to represent Great Britain in Paralympic equestrianism. As she says, "Just because it's an ambitious goal doesn't mean it's impossible."

BORN DECEMBER 3, 2001
UNITED KINGDOM

"I LIKE PROVING PEOPLE WRONG."
—TEGAN VINCENT-COOKE

ILLUSTRATION BY
DEANDRA HODGE

YUSRA MARDINI

SWIMMER

Once there was a girl named Yusra who believed swimming could save her life—and it did! Yusra grew up in Damascus, Syria, where she and her sister swam a lot at the local swimming pool with their father. But when Yusra was 13, a civil war erupted in Syria. Her home and her favorite pool were destroyed. She and her family knew they had to flee.

A few years later, in the summer of 2015, Yusra and her sister joined a group of refugees trying to get to safety in Europe. They'd made it from Syria to Lebanon and then to Turkey. Next, they planned to take a small boat to get to Greece. There was only enough room for six or seven people on the boat, but Yusra found 20 people aboard, all packed together. After they set out, the boat's motor broke down! Yusra knew what to do.

Yusra, her sister, and two other passengers jumped overboard and started swimming, pushing the boat along. It was terrifying. Each time they lifted an arm out of the water or took a breath, they knew so many lives depended on them. They swam for more than three hours, pulling the boat through the Aegean Sea until, finally, they reached the shore!

As soon as Yusra settled into her new life in Europe, she dove back into the water. Only this time, it was a swimming pool in Germany, and she was training for the Olympics. In 2016, she competed in Rio as part of the first-ever Refugee Olympic Team. As the team entered the arena, the fans roared. It had taken so much for the brave athletes to get there. "The whole stadium stood up," she recalled. "I would not trade this moment for anything in my life."

Five years later, at the Tokyo Olympics opening ceremony, Yusra fulfilled another wish: she proudly carried the flag for the refugee team!

BORN MARCH 5, 1998

SYRIA

ILLUSTRATION BY
JESSICA COOPER

"I TELL MY STORY BECAUSE I
WANT PEOPLE TO UNDERSTAND
THAT SPORT SAVED MY LIFE."
—YUSRA MARDINI

WRITE YOUR STORY

_____

_____

_____

_____

_____

_____

_____

_____

_____

_____

_____

_____

_____

_____

_____

_____

DRAW YOUR PORTRAIT

WHAT KIND OF CHAMPION ARE YOU?

1. WHICH WORDS DESCRIBE YOU THE MOST?

A. Energetic, always on the go

B. Smart, patient

C. Flexible, fearless

D. Daring, curious

2. WHEN YOU SEE AN OPEN FIELD, WHAT DO YOU DO?

A. Run through it as fast as you can

B. Think, *Dang it, where's my ball?*

C. Do flips and cartwheels

D. Start looking for four-leaf clovers

3. BEING PART OF A SPORTS TEAM . . .

A. . . . makes you so, so happy!

B. . . . means you have to show up on time for practice.

C. . . . is fun, but you prefer exercising on your own.

D. . . . sounds hard.

4. ONE OF YOUR ALL-TIME FAVORITE SPORTS HEROES IS _____.

A. Flo Jo

B. Naomi Osaka

C. Simone Biles

D. Lindsey Vonn

5. HOW MUCH TIME DO YOU SPEND PLAYING SPORTS EACH WEEK?

A. 15 to 20 hours

B. 10 to 15 hours

C. 5 to 10 hours

D. Somewhere between 0 and 40. Time flies when you're having fun.

6. WHEN YOU'RE NOT PLAYING SPORTS, YOU LIKE TO _____.

A. watch sports on TV

B. play board games

C. paint your nails

D. melt cheese on things

7. YOUR FAVORITE FOOD IS _____.

A. a protein smoothie

B. a veggie burrito

C. yogurt and berries

D. anything with noodles

8. IF YOU COULD HAVE ANY SUPERPOWER IT WOULD BE _____.

A. super speed

B. the power of invisibility

C. the ability to shape-shift

D. the ability to fly

9. IF AN EXTRA HOUR WAS ADDED TO TODAY, WHAT WOULD YOU DO?

A. Go for a run

B. Dance like nobody's watching

C. Check your clocks. (How on Earth could there be an extra hour?)

D. Take a nap

10. WHAT'S YOUR FAVORITE PART ABOUT PLAYING GAMES?

A. Figuring out the rules and scoring points!

B. Strategizing your next move. Sometimes you've planned three moves ahead!

C. Playing each turn and moving through each level with style.

D. Trying out new things.

Check out the answer key on page 62!

TRAINING TIME

Athletes have lots of techniques for keeping their minds and bodies fit. Here are some activities you can try too!

EVERYDAY OBSTACLE COURSE

Are you as speedy as Allyson Felix? Can you jump as far as Fleur Jong? Use your yard or a nearby park as your own training ground.

1. Look around and find a bench, fence, or cool-looking tree. How long does it take you to run there and back? Have a grown-up time you. Do three timed trials to set your best time. Try again next week and see how you improve!

2. Find two items. They can be leaves, rocks, acorns, or items you brought outside with you. Place them on the ground about a foot apart. Can you jump that distance? Keep moving the objects farther apart to test your long jump skills. Be sure to get a running start!

DON'T BURST MY BUBBLE!

When a young Serena Williams practiced tennis, her father would ask kids to yell and boo so she could learn to ignore distractions. Are you able to focus when there are things going on around you?

1. Blow up a balloon, then tie it closed. Throw it in the air. When it starts to float down, hit it again. Don't let it touch the ground!

2. Ask a friend or family member to distract you by singing loudly or trying to make you laugh. How long can you keep the balloon in the air?

3. Challenge yourself with new rules! Try alternating hands or how you hit the balloon. First, hit it with the palm of your hand, then the top of your hand, then the palm of your hand again.

GO TO **REBELGIRLS.COM** OR THE **REBEL GIRLS APP** AND CHOOSE A PODCAST EPISODE OR APP STORY. PRACTICE STRETCHES WHILE YOU LISTEN TO MORE TALES OF AWESOME ATHLETES.

WATER BOTTLE WORKOUT

When COVID-19 struck and airports shut down, weightlifter Hidilyn Diaz got stuck far away from home. She had to get creative to work out indoors. You can too! Fill up two water bottles of the same size and try these simple arm exercises.

1. Hold a bottle in each hand and put your arms straight down by your sides. Bend your arms forward to lift the bottles up to your shoulders. Then return your hands to your sides. Do that 8 times.
2. Return your arms to your sides. Now keep your arms straight as you lift them out to the sides until the water bottles are shoulder height. Slowly return your arms to your sides. Repeat 8 times.
3. Bend your arms so you're holding the water bottles close to your shoulders. Lift the bottles up in the air until your arms are straight. Slowly bend your arms to bring the bottles back down. Repeat 8 times.
4. Do this entire workout 3 times. Then, rest and drink some water!

EMBRACE YOUR INNER FLAMINGO!

Gymnasts like Simone Biles and Suni Lee practice their balance all the time so they are ready to compete on the beam. Are you ready for some balance training?

1. Stand on one leg with the other out in front of you. Hold your arms out at your sides. Count to 20. Do it on the other leg.
2. Grab a pillow or a sofa cushion and put it on the floor. (Make sure there's nothing sharp or pointy around you, in case you lose your balance!) Repeat step 1 while standing on the cushion.
3. Place something about one foot tall on the ground (a teddy bear, a stack of books, a water bottle, etc.) Take one big step back from your object. Stand on one leg with your other leg out behind you. Hold your arms out at your sides and lean down until you can touch your object. Still balancing on one leg, straighten back up. Repeat 5 times. Then try it on the other leg.

ANSWER KEY

MOSTLY As

You're a SPEEDY SPORTSTER! Your energy is boundless, and you inspire everyone around you to shout hooray! When you are in the zone, there is literally no stopping you. Make sure to hydrate, and check out your fellow champions LISA LESLIE and MEGAN RAPINOE.

MOSTLY Bs

You're a POWERHOUSE WITH A PURPOSE! You keep your eye on the ball, and your brain works just as hard as your feet! Your stamina and skill are superb. Competitors need to watch out for you and your strategic mind! Make sure to read about champions TEGAN VINCENT-COOKE and SERENA WILLIAMS.

MOSTLY Cs

Hello, DYNAMO DANCER! You are made of music, and you set the beat with every spin, leap, and lunge. Whether you're jumping off the balance beam or practicing your triple lutz on the ice, you go to the edge of fear and find your fun. And for that, your fans applaud you! Find strength and inspiration in your champion sisters SUNI LEE and MICHELLE KWAN.

MOSTLY Ds

Watch out, world! Here comes an ARDENT ADVENTURER! You are fueled by curiosity (and noodles!) and love to follow the wind whichever way it turns! Sometimes this means you may get distracted, but it also means you find the most delicious-looking sunsets and may have the coolest sneakers in town. Enjoy every second of exploration, and soon you'll be just like champions SKY BROWN and LINA and SANNA EL KOTT HELANDER.

MORE STORIES

Meet more amazing Rebels in other Rebel Girls books. And check out the Rebel Girls Dream On app to listen to more stories and do fun activities.

THE ILLUSTRATORS

Twenty extraordinary female and nonbinary artists from all over the world illustrated the portraits in this book. Here are their names.

ANDRESSA MEISSNER, BRAZIL, 23

ANNALISA VENTURA, ITALY, 35

CAMILLA RU, UK, 45

CARMEN CASADO, SPAIN, 43

DANIELLE ELYSSE MANN, USA, 51

DEANDRA HODGE, USA, 21, 53

ELINE VAN DAM, NETHERLANDS, 47

JENNIFER BERGLUND, SWEDEN, 31

JESSICA COOPER, USA, 55

JULIETTE LÉVEILLÉ, FRANCE, 7

KATE PRIOR, USA, 49

KIM HOLT, USA, 9, 33, 37

LILY KIM QIAN, CANADA, 39

LYDIA MBA, SPAIN, 15

MAYA MCKIBBIN, CANADA, 13

MIA SAINE, USA, 19

MONICA MIKAI, USA, 25, 27

SALINI PERERA, CANADA, 17, 41

SOL COTTI, ARGENTINA, 11

XUAN LOC XUAN, VIETNAM, 29

ABOUT REBEL GIRLS

REBEL GIRLS is a global, multi-platform empowerment brand dedicated to helping raise the most inspired and confident global generation of girls through content, experiences, products, and community. Originating from an international best-selling children's book, Rebel Girls amplifies stories of real-life, extraordinary women throughout history, geography, and field of excellence. With a growing community of nearly 20 million self-identified Rebel Girls spanning more than 100 countries, the brand engages with Generation Alpha through its book series, award-winning podcast, events, and merchandise.

Join the Rebel Girls' community:

- Facebook: facebook.com/rebelgirls
- Instagram: @rebelgirls
- Twitter: @rebelgirlsbook
- Web: rebelgirls.com
- Podcast: rebelgirls.com/podcast

If you liked this book, please take a moment to review it wherever you prefer!